# Shake It Up

Cheers!

How many pool parties
will it take to get through
these recipes? Let's just see!

Thanks for your
friendship & your
spontaneous, fun
nature!
love,
Jimmi

# Shake It Up

## Chic Cocktails & Girly Drinks

A Chicklits Book

CONARI PRESS

First published in 2005 by Conari Press,
an imprint of Red Wheel/Weiser, LLC
York Beach, ME
With offices at:
368 Congress Street
Boston, MA 02210
*www.redwheelweiser.com*

Acknowledgments on page 64
1-57324-223-3

Typeset in TheSans, SignPainter, Ogre, Parade, Pike, Cafe Mimi,
and Felt-Tip Woman by Jill Feron, FeronDesign

Printed in China
CC

11 10 09 08 07 06 05
 8  7  6  5  4  3  2  1

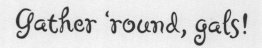
# Gather 'round, gals!

All the problems of the world can be solved with just two ingredients—friendship and the right libation. From the common cold (hot brandy with lemon) to the morning blahs (Bloody Mary, even Virgin!) to a broken heart (one bottle of wine plus one best friend), there is no problem too great to be resolved through sheer chick-power. So, pull out your planner and start dialing. Herein is a host(ess) of recipes, ideas, and terrific trivia to help you master the art of the cocktail and blend up a batch of bliss.

A party girl always makes sure she and fellow chicks have eaten to help metabolize AND a responsible hostess makes sure guests have a safe ride home or warm spot on the couch. Many of the drinks herein can also be made alcohol-free. The right beverage for the right occasion is the key!

Don't forget, everything tastes better with your friends at your side!

"There comes a time in every woman's life when the only thing that helps is a glass of champagne."
—BETTE DAVIS

The invention of champagne, circa 1700 by a monk named Dom Perignon, was a major event in chick history. It is said that he cried out to his fellow monks, "Come quickly, I am tasting the stars." Some savvy chicks even include "the bubbly" in their beauty regimen—one flute adds just the right amount of sparkle.

# Sunset Champagne Cocktails

1 quart lemonade
1 16-ounce jar Maraschino cherries
2 bottles of champagne, chilled

Chill the lemonade overnight in a glass pitcher. Just before setting out on the buffet table, pour the cherries and their syrup into the lemonade. Set out both the pitcher and the champagne on the buffet table; guests can add juice to the champagne to taste. Makes 18-20 servings.

## A Toast to Trivia

*Champagne gets you drunk faster than still wine because the carbon monoxide in the bubbles moves alcohol more quickly into your bloodstream.*

# Some like it salty . . .

## Margarita

2 ounce tequila
$\frac{1}{2}$ ounce triple sec
1 ounce lime juice
salt

Rub rim of cocktail glass with lime juice, and dip rim in salt. Pour tequila, triple sec, and lime juice over ice and shake. Strain into salt-rimmed glass and serve.

A pitcher of margaritas, a bowl of chips, and some tangy salsa is a guaranteed conversation starter. In fact, this is the makings for an instant party!

**Oprah Winfrey** credits **Julia Roberts** with making the **best margaritas** in the business.

# A Toast to Trivia

**LIZ TAYLOR** has earned a permanent place in chick history for her talent, beauty, charity, and occasional outrageousness.

✳ ✳ ✳

In her old drinking days, Taylor's favorite drink was a **CHOCOLATE MARTINI,** which she and Rock Hudson concocted on the set of *Giant*.

# Chocolate Martini

2 ounces vodka
2 ounces crème de cacao

Pour ingredients into a shaker filled with ice. Shake, then pour into a martini glass. Garnish with a cherry.

\* \* \*

*This is a delicious treat, for when you're "on location," a long way from home with a handsome guy pal.*

# EVER WONDER WHY WINE GLASSES COME IN DIFFERENT ShApeS?

There's a real science to it. Each type of glass is made to accentuate a certain type of wine's bouquet or bubbles, then deliver the wine to the appropriate portion of the tongue (the taste buds for salty, sweet, sour, and bitter are in different parts of the tongue).

# Retail Therapy Tip

Some bargain babes and vintage vixens prowl **thrift stores** and **yard sales** in search of 25-cent treasures—great old goblets, fabulous flutes, and sassy snifters in unusual shapes, sizes, and colors. **Far lovelier** and way more **interesting** than the perfect set of wine glasses everyone *else* has.

# Mardi Gras means "Fat Tuesday,"

the last day before Ash Wednesday, when the Lenten season begins. Depending on how early or late Easter is each year, Mardi Gras can be celebrated in March or April. The first Mardi Gras celebration was in New Orleans in 1827. In the olden times, people dressed in animal skin, pelted each other with bunches of flowers, and drank wine. Also called Carnival, this rite of spring is celebrated all over the world. Mardi Gras was made for friends getting together—let the good times roll!

# Mardi Gras Punch

1 ice ring (giant ice cube made in a
    Bundt or ring mold)
1 40-ounce bottle grape juice
1 48-ounce can unsweetened pineapple juice
1 750-ml bottle vodka
2 oranges, thinly sliced
2 lemons, thinly sliced
2 limes, thinly sliced
1 2-liter bottle lemon-lime soda

Place ice ring in bottom of big glass or clear plastic
punch bowl. Add liquids in order given. Float slices
of oranges and limes on top. Makes enough for a
party!

## SOLVE THE "DESIGNATED DRIVER DILEMMA"

WITH A GIRLS' NIGHT IN AT YOUR HOUSE. POP SOME CORN, ORDER A PIZZA, AND RENT OLD MOVIES AND GET READY TO LAUGH UNTIL YOU CRY.

## THIS CHICK-TESTED CONCOCTION IS A GREAT ACCOMPANIMENT . . .

# Loopy Laura Martinis

Absolute Currant
Pink lemonade
Squeeze of fresh lemon

Mix this up until it's yummy (about 1 part vodka to 3 parts lemonade is a good start). Take everyone's keys at the door. This cocktail makes your gathering an automatic slumber party. If you don't believe us, ask Laura.

# This gal's choice of venom

Together we crewed an all-women sailboat, earning us the nickname "Ladies of the Lake." At holiday time, we rented a limousine and cruised around, viewing the Christmas lights. We have found that July is the hardest month to gather everyone together, so we suspend our gatherings in lieu of family vacations for that month. We do our part to support local restaurants and we're not afraid to have a cocktail. **Our favorite libation is a SNAKEBITE—equal parts tequila and peppermint schnapps, sipped from little mugs.**

—SHERYL ANN LEE, AKA DUFF

It's not a drink for sissies.

# No Wimpy Umbrellas for Her:

Haven't you always wondered where the term
**COCKTAIL** came from?

> *WONDER NO MORE.* A barmaid in Elmsford,
> New York, by the name of Betsy Flanagan used
> to decorate her drinks with a **ROOSTER FEATHER.**

One day a customer asked for
> *"ONE OF THOSE COCK TAILS"*
> and the name stuck—and spread.

*Siberian sirens need
something to keep them warm
now that fur is so* **outré!**

# Russian Huntress

Crushed ice
2 ½ shots Kahlua
1 to 1½ shots vodka
Half-and-half to top the glass
Approximately ¼ shot Galliano liqueur

Fill a highball glass almost to the top with crushed ice. Pour in Kahlua, vodka, and enough half-and-half to almost top the glass. Pour in the Galliano float and stir.

*Serve with care: guaranteed to incite the wild woman in each who drinks this*

"If I hadn't
had them,
I would have
had some made."

—DOLLY PARTON ON HER SIZABLE BREASTS

# Buttery Nipple

½ ounce Butterscotch Schnapps
½ once Bailey's Irish Cream

Pour the Butterscotch Schnapps into a shot glass.
Spoon in Bailey's Irish Cream.

This layered shot is delicious!

"Love is an exploding cigar we willingly smoke."

—LINDA BARRY, CARTOONIST

# Between the Sheets

2 ounces light rum
2 ounces brandy
2 ounces Cointreau
2 teaspoons lemon juice

In a cocktail shaker, half-full of ice cubes, combine all the ingredients. Shake to mix. Strain the mixture into two highball glasses, filled almost to the top with ice cubes. Makes 2 cocktails.

Before the four chicks from *Sex and The City* stormed Manhattan, wicked wit Dorothy Parker ruled New York City from the Round Table at the Algonquin Hotel.

This legendary and literary place still makes remarkable martinis.

*"One more drink and I'd be under my host."*

—DOROTHY PARKER

# Appletini

2 ounces Vodka
1 ounce Apple Pucker
A dash of pineapple juice
A dash of sour mix

Combine ingredients in mixing tin over ice, shake
or stir. Strain into chilled cocktail glass and garnish
with a slice of Granny Smith apple and a cherry.

# Are most of your girlfriends on a diet?

Reward them and support them
with this almost entirely
guilt-free chick drink.

# Moscow Mule

2 ounces vodka
1 ounce lime juice
Diet ginger ale

Pour vodka in a low-ball cocktail glass with ice.
Add lime juice and top off with ginger ale.

# The Perfect Pear

You know, there are some things
the French simply do better.
This is definitely one of those things:

Have you ever seen those **bottles** of
French brandy with the **WHOLE pear inside**
and wondered how it got in there?

## Here's the answer:

French farmers tie bottles onto pear
blossoms and the pear actually **grows inside**
the glass. Then they add the brandy.

# We'll Always Have Manhattan

## A Toast to Trivia

The Manhattan was invented by Jennie Jerome, a beautiful New York socialite in the 1870s who broke the hearts of American men when she went off to England to marry a lord. Lord Churchill, that is; Jennie would become Winston Churchill's mother.

# Manhattan

4 ounces blended whiskey
1 ounce sweet vermouth
4 dashes bitters
2 maraschino cherries

Chill two cocktail glasses. In a cocktail shaker, half full of ice cubes, combine all the ingredients except the maraschino cherries. Shake to mix. Strain the mixture into the glasses. Garnish each drink with a maraschino cherry. Makes 2 cocktails.

# And, Don't Forget
## Long Island

# Long Island Iced Tea

3/4 ounce gin
3/4 ounce light rum
3/4 ounce tequila
3/4 ounce vodka
A dash of cola
Lemon or lime to garnish

This drink is in and of itself a party.

Pour all liquors into a highball glass half-full of ice and stir. Add cola for color and garnish with lemon or lime.

# Suggestion:

invite your friends over for some iced tea on the back porch followed by a nap.

*Ahhh...*

# Swimming Pool

3/4 ounce vodka
3/4 ounce white rum
3/4 ounce blue curacao
2 ounces coconut cream
4 ounces pineapple juice

Pour all ingredients into a shaker filled with ice. Shake and strain into a martini glass. Garnish with a pineapple wedge and an orange wheel.

# On the Beach

The "tiki drink" renaissance and the grand tradition of college "spring break" has given rise to many cocktails with wildly suggestive names. Here is a most ironic take on a classic, "Sex on the Beach," —a virgin version!

    1 part Orange Juice
    1 part Cranberry juice
    1 ounce of peach nectar
    a healthy splash of Grenadine.

    Mix this up and pour it over ice,
    garnish with pineapple chunks,
    and serve.

# A Toast to Trivia

## Greece, *then*

In ancient Greece and Rome, women weren't allowed to drink alcohol, except for *passum*, a sweet wine made from raisins. And they weren't fooling around; in the second century A.D., husbands were known to murder their wives if they were caught sneaking down into the wine cellar.

# A Toast to Trivia

## Grape Gals, *now*

For years, the wine industry was dominated by men. One of the pioneers in women and wine-making was Isabel Simi who inherited the Simi Winery in Healdsburg, California and established one of the first tasting rooms in California. Isabel welcomed other women into the industry, including Mary Ann Graf who founded "Vinquiry" and left a legacy of wonderful vintages and laid new ground for "women in wine."

# Fire Sign Wine

1 bottle (1.5 liter, 54 fluid ounces) full-bodied
 red wine (Burgundy or Beaujolais Nouveau
 works nicely)

3/4 cups sugar

3 cinnamon sticks, one partially grated

12 whole cloves and a pinch of ground cloves

1/2 teaspoon ground allspice

1 orange, juice and rind

1 lemon, juice and rind

1 1/2 to 2 cups vodka (the stormier the weather,
 the more spirits are needed)

In a large, nonreactive saucepan, stir the wine, sugar, and spices together, grating part of one cinnamon stick over the mixture. Heat, covered, over very low heat while you cut the lemon and orange into 6 to 8 sections, squeeze the juice into the wine, and drop the segments of rind into the pot. Simmer for about 20 minutes or until wine is burning hot to the touch, but do not let boil.

Add the vodka. When the potion is again almost too hot to taste-test, it is ready to drink. Serve in heat-tempered punch cups or glass mugs. Warms up 4 to 6.

## *Oatmeal Cookie*

2 ounces Goldschlager or Hotdam
2 ounces Butterscotch Schnapps
2 ounces Bailey's Irish Crème

Combine all ingredients with ice and shake. Strain and serve in shot glass. Makes two to three shots.

# Butter Scotch Bliss Cookies

1 cup softened butter
1 cup brown sugar
1/2 cup granulated sugar
2 eggs
2 teaspoons vanilla
2 1/4 cups all-purpose flour
1 teaspoon baking soda
1 teaspoon salt
12 ounces butterscotch chips

Cream the butter until soft, add sugar, and cream until light and fluffy. Beat in the eggs and vanilla. Sift the flour with baking soda and salt. Scoop up rounded tablespoons two inches apart on a cookie sheet that has been greased. Bake at 375 degrees for ten to fifteen minutes. If you like your cookies yummy and moist, take them out sooner and plate them immediately. You can get about 50 cookies from this batch.

On
Occasion

This is the perfect punch to put together for a bridal shower, college graduation, or other special chick occasion.

Easy to make, it tastes simply wonderful.

Other chick celebration occasions might be a well-deserved promotion, quitting the job you hate, a long-overdue break-up, or finding the best pair of shoes ever!

# Champagne Brunch Punch

4 cans frozen orange juice
1 bottle white wine
1 cup curacao or triple sec
ice
3 bottles of champagne

Pour first three ingredients over ice in punch bowl.
Just before serving, add the champagne.

Rent the DVDs of the first year of *Sex and the City* and gather the girls together for some cosmos. The Fab Four are a true celebration of bonds of friendship, chick-style.

# The Classic Cosmopolitan

4 parts vodka
2 parts triple sec
2 parts cranberry juice
1 part fresh lime juice

Pour ingredients into a shaker with ice. Shake it all together, and strain into martini glasses. Garnish with a twisted sliver of lime or lemon peel.

*"Miranda was a huge fan of the Yankees.*
*I was a huge fan of being anywhere you could smoke*
*and drink at two in the afternoon without judgment."*
—Carrie from *Sex and the City*

*Sex and the City* was a huge hit in China via bootlegged tapes. An enterprising Shanghai television station has come up with its own version entitled *Hot Ladies*, where a feisty foursome drink **"SHANGHAI COSMOS."** To make this exotic elixir, fill a shaker with ice and add one ounce each of Cranberry juice, Choya plum wine, and vodka with just a splash of pineapple juice and lime. Shake and then strain into a cold martini glass. Topped with soda and garnished with a twist of lemon, these are wickedly delicious.

# Irish Coffee

coffee
brown sugar
1 jigger Irish Whiskey
heavy cream

Fill glasses with hot water to preheat, then empty. Pour piping hot coffee into warmed glass until it is about ¾ full. Add 1 tablespoon brown sugar and stir until completely dissolved. Blend in Irish Whiskey. Top with a collar of slightly whipped heavy cream by pouring gently over a spoon. Enjoy while piping hot.

This Irish Whiskey drink was invented in World War II after some weary travelers landed in Shannon, Ireland, after one of the bumpiest rides in history. The mix of coffee, fine Irish Whiskey, sugar, and heavy whipped cream perked them up immediately. Intrigued, a bartender flew to Ireland in 1952, learned the trade secret recipe and brought it back to San Francisco's Buena Vista Saloon in San Francisco's Fisherman's Wharf. The Buena Vista still serves about 2000 Irish Coffees a day and, boy, are they good.

# A Toast to Trivia

Kubaba of Kish was a Sumerian woman who ran a beer tavern in 2500 B.C. and eventually became queen. Ancient Sumerians loved their suds and even had a common saying:

*"Beer makes the liver happy and fills the heart with joy."*

Beer has been made since 6000 B.C. (although it did go out of vogue for a while because the ancient Greeks thought it caused leprosy), and women made and sold most of it, at least in Mesopotamia. They drank their share of it too, even the priestesses at the temple. Until modern sanitation, beer was much safer than water, and in northern Europe it provided much of the nutrition in daily diets until as late as the seventeenth century.

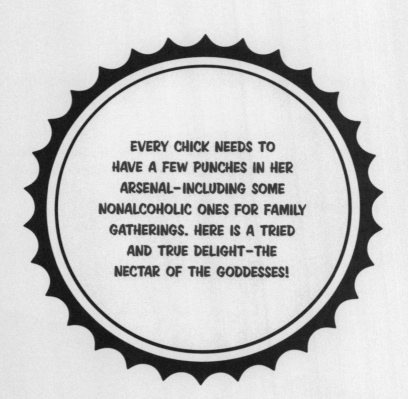

EVERY CHICK NEEDS TO HAVE A FEW PUNCHES IN HER ARSENAL—INCLUDING SOME NONALCOHOLIC ONES FOR FAMILY GATHERINGS. HERE IS A TRIED AND TRUE DELIGHT—THE NECTAR OF THE GODDESSES!

# Ambrosia Punch

1 20-ounce can crushed pineapple, undrained
1 15-ounce can of cream of coconut
2 cups apricot nectar, chilled
2 cups orange juice, chilled
1 liter club soda, chilled
1 ½ cups light rum
  * for a nonalcoholic punch, substitute an equal
  amount of tangerine soda for the rum

In a blender, puree pineapple and cream of coconut
until smooth. In a punch bowl, combine the puree,
nectar, juice, and rum. Mix well. Just before serving,
add club soda and serve over ice. Serves 12.

*If you like Piña Coladas . . .*

# Piña Colada

3 ounces rum
3 ounces cream of coconut
3 ounces pineapple juice
6 ice cubes

Put all ingredients into a blender and blend until smooth. Makes 2 drinks.

**PIÑA COLADAS ARE A *CLASSIC* CHICK COCKTAIL.** Sometimes, after a hot day at the beach or a hot night on the dance floor, nothing else but this long, tall, fabulous froth will do.

This is **NOT** the Jell-O®
treat your grandma made for
the family reunion picnics!

Though for some they conjure up images of drunken frat parties, we're huge fans of Jell-O® shooters. They're inexpensive, easy to make, tasty, and because of the array of colors available, adaptable for almost any party. We've made black and orange Jell-O® shooters for Halloween, and red and blue for the Fourth of July.

To make Jell-O® shooters, simply replace half of the cold water called for in the recipe on the Jell-O® box with vodka. If there will be kids or non-drinkers, make "virgin" shooters for them.

# A Toast to Trivia

Queen Elizabeth I so loved vanilla that in her later years she would only consume food and drink laced with the stuff. (Yes, vanilla extract contains alcohol.)

Many a southern belle has ditched the juleps and moved onto Vanilla Cokes. Yum!

# Vanilla Coke

1 ½ ounces Southern Comfort
1 ½ ounces Vanilla Liqueur
1 can Cola

Put some ice in a highball glass. Pour in Southern Comfort and Vanilla Liqueur. Fill rest of the way with Cola.

## CRAFTY CHICK TIPS –

make your own vanilla extract; it is SO easy:

**INGREDIENTS:** one vanilla bean, 4 ounces of vodka and a small, colored and stoppered jar.

Cut the vanilla bean in half and insert it in the jar. Pour in the vodka and store in a cool, dark place for at least one month. The longer you leave it, the stronger your extract will be. If the jar is pretty, put a label and a ribbon on it and it makes a fantastic gift.

Invite your fellow chicks
over with some "Homebrew."
Makes a great gift, too.

# Home-brew "Kahlua"

4 cups water
5 cups sugar
1 jar (2 ounces) instant coffee (Yuban works well)
4 cups vodka
1 large vanilla bean, cut into pieces or
3 tablespoons pure vanilla extract

In a large heavy saucepan, bring water to a boil; add sugar and coffee and leave over heat for 3 to 4 minutes more. Remove from heat and let cool *completely*.

When mixture has cooled, add vodka and vanilla. Pour into a glass 1-gallon container and let season for at least three weeks to a month, shaking once a day. Strain the elixir into a decorative decanter and enjoy as you please. Makes ½ gallon of home-brew.

**VIRGIN or BLOODY, this elixir wakes up a Sunday.**

## Sunday Bloody Mary Mix

1 can (46 ounces) tomato juice
1 teaspoon celery salt
3/4 teaspoon black pepper
1 tablespoon lemon juice
2 tablespoons Worcestershire sauce
2 teaspoons horseradish sauce
5 dashes Tabasco sauce (some like it hot!)
    or to taste

1 ½ to 2 shots of the best vodka you can
   afford per drink
Old Bay seasoning to taste
Olives and celery, for garnish

Mix thoroughly in a large container that can be sealed
tightly and always shake before using.

Mix with the quantity of vodka that you think a Bloody
Mary should have in it, garnish with olives and celery, and
don't make any plans to drive anywhere in the near future.

Makes enough for 6 jumbo Bloody Marys.
For a Virgin Mary, simply eliminate the vodka.

R-e-l-a-x... it's Sunday!

Grateful acknowledgment is made to the following for permission to reprint material copyrighted by them. All reprinted by permission of Red Wheel/Weiser.

Alicia Alvrez, *The Ladies' Room Reader*. Boston, MA: Conari Press, an imprint of Red Wheel/Weiser, 2000.
    Liz Taylor Trivia p. 10
    Cocktail Trivia p. 19
    Manhattan Trivia p. 32
    Greek Wine Trivia p. 38
    Beer Trivia p. 51–52
    Queen Elizabeth Trivia p. 58

Alicia Alvrez, *The Ladies' Room Reader Revisited*. Boston, MA: Conari Press, an imprint of Red Wheel/Weiser, 2002.
    Wine Glass Trivia p. 12
    Pear Trivia p. 31

Ame Mahler Beanland and Emily Miles Terry, *It's a Chick Thing*. Boston, MA: Conari Press, an imprint of Red Wheel/Weiser, 2000.
    Loopy Laura Martinis p. 17
    Venom Drinks p. 18
    The Classic Cosmopolitan p. 46
    Jell-O® Shots p. 57

Margie Lapanja, *Romancing the Stove*. Boston, MA: Conari Press, an imprint of Red Wheel/Weiser, 1998.
    Russian Huntress p. 20–21
    Fire Sign Wine p. 40–41
    Home-brew "Kahlua" p. 61
    Sunday Bloody Mary Mix p. 62–63

Nina Lesowitz & Lara Morris Starr, *The Party Girl Cookbook*. Boston, MA: Conari Press, an imprint of Red Wheel/Weiser, 1999.
    Sunset Champagne Cocktails p. 7
    Mardi Gras Punch p. 15
    Between the Sheets p. 25
    Manhattan p. 33
    Champagne Brunch Punch p. 45
    Irish Coffee p. 48
    Ambrosia Punch p. 53
    Piña Colada p. 55

Autumn Stephens, *Out of the Mouths of Babes*. Boston, MA: Conari Press, an imprint of Red Wheel/Weiser, 2000.
    Linda Barry Quote p. 24